All scripture quotations marked NKJV are taken from the New King James Version®. Copyright © 1982 by Thomas Nelson. Used by permission. All rights reserved.

Grieving in the Holy Spirit. Copyright © 2022 All rights reserved – Arletha Orr

No portion of this book may be reproduced or transmitted in any form or by any means, graphic, electronic, or mechanical, including photocopying, recording, taping, or by information storage retrieval system without the written permission of the publisher.

Please direct all copyright inquiries to:
Kingdom Trailblazers
c/o Author Copyrights
Post Office Box 767
Flora, MS 39071

Hardback ISBN: 979-8-9865905-4-7
Design: Kingdom Trailblazers Publishing
Printed in the United States.

www.iStillLoveMe.com

Five Stages of Grief

Five Stages of Grief

Denial

Denial is the first of the five stages of grief. It helps us to survive the loss. In this stage, the world becomes meaningless and overwhelming. Life makes no sense. We are in a state of shock and denial. We go numb. We wonder how we can go on, if we can go on, why we should go on. We try to find a way to simply get through each day. Denial helps us to pace our feelings of grief. As you accept the reality of the loss, you begin the healing process. You are becoming stronger!

Anger

Anger is a necessary stage of the healing process. Be willing to feel your anger, even though it may seem endless. The more you truly feel it, the more it will begin to dissipate and the more you will heal. The truth is that anger has no limits. It can extend not only to your friends, the doctors, your family, yourself and your loved one who died, but also to God. You may ask, "Where is God in this? Underneath anger is pain, your pain. It is natural to feel deserted and abandoned, but we live in a society that fears anger. Anger is strength and it can be an anchor.

Five Stages of Grief

Bargaining

Before a loss, it seems like you will do anything if only your loved one would be spared. After a loss, bargaining may take the form of a temporary truce. We become lost in a maze of "If only..." or "What if..." statements. We want life returned to what it was; we want our loved one restored. We want to go back in time: find the tumor sooner, recognize the illness more quickly, stop the accident from happening...if only, if only, if only. Guilt is often bargaining's companion.

Depression

After bargaining, our attention moves squarely into the present. Empty feelings present themselves, and grief enters our lives on a deeper level, deeper than we ever imagined. This depressive stage feels as though it will last forever. It's important to understand that this depression is not a sign of mental illness. It is the appropriate response to a great loss. We withdraw from life, left in a fog of intense sadness, wondering, perhaps, if there is any point in going on alone? Why go on at all? The loss of a loved one is a very depressing situation, and depression is a normal and appropriate response.

Five Stages of Grief

Acceptance

Acceptance is often confused with the notion of being "all right" or "OK" with what has happened. This is not the case. Most people don't ever feel OK or all right about the loss of a loved one. This stage is about accepting the reality that our loved one is physically gone and recognizing that this new reality is the permanent reality. We will never like this reality or make it OK, but eventually we accept it. We learn to live with it. It is the new norm with which we must learn to live.

The definition for the five stages of grief came from the following source: https://grief.com/the-five-stages-of-grief/.

Five Stages of Grief

Describe how each stage has affected you.

DENIAL

_____
_____
_____
_____
_____

ANGER

_____
_____
_____
_____
_____

BARGAINING

_____
_____
_____
_____
_____

www.iStillLoveMe.com

Five Stages of Grief

Describe how each stage has affected you.

DEPRESSION

_____
_____
_____
_____
_____
_____

ACCEPTANCE

_____
_____
_____
_____
_____
_____

What stage do you feel like you're in now?

Denial   **Anger**   **Bargaining**   **Depression**   **Acceptance**

Feelings Journal

Date

My flesh and my heart may fail, but God is the strength of my heart and my portion forever. Psalm 73:26 NKJV

I feel sad because

_____
_____
_____
_____
_____
_____

Today I remembered

_____
_____
_____
_____
_____
_____

The things I miss most

_____
_____
_____

www.iStillLoveMe.com

Feelings Journal

Date

Jesus said to her, "I am the resurrection and the life. The one who believes in me will live, even though they die; and whoever lives by believing in me will never die. Do you believe this?" John 11:25-26 NKJV

I feel sad because

_____
_____
_____
_____
_____
_____

Today I remembered

_____
_____
_____
_____
_____
_____

The things I miss most

_____
_____
_____

www.iStillLoveMe.com

Feelings Journal

Date

If we live, we live for the Lord; and if we die, we die for the Lord. So, whether we live or die, we belong to the Lord. Romans 14:8 NKJV

I feel sad because

_____
_____
_____
_____
_____

Today I remembered

_____
_____
_____
_____
_____
_____

The things I miss most

_____
_____
_____

www.iStillLoveMe.com

Feelings Journal

Date

He will wipe every tear from their eyes. There will be no more death' or mourning or crying or pain, for the old order of things has passed away. Revelation 21:4 NKJV

I feel sad because

_____
_____
_____
_____
_____
_____

Today I remembered

_____
_____
_____
_____
_____
_____

The things I miss most

_____
_____
_____

www.iStillLoveMe.com

Feelings Journal

Date

The LORD is close to the brokenhearted and saves those who are crushed in spirit. Psalms 34:18 NKJV

I feel sad because

Today I remembered

The things I miss most

www.iStillLoveMe.com

Focusing on Your Feelings

When I learned of the death I felt

_____
_____
_____
_____
_____
_____

My reaction to the death was

_____
_____
_____
_____
_____
_____

After the death I

_____
_____
_____
_____
_____
_____

Feelings Journal

Date

He heals the brokenhearted and binds up their wounds.
Psalms 147:3 NKJV

I feel sad because

_____
_____
_____
_____
_____
_____

Today I remembered

_____
_____
_____
_____
_____
_____

The things I miss most

_____
_____
_____

www.iStillLoveMe.com

Feelings Journal

Date

Do not let your hearts be troubled. You believe in God; believe also in me. John 14:1 NKJV

I feel sad because

_____
_____
_____
_____
_____
_____

Today I remembered

_____
_____
_____
_____
_____
_____

The things I miss most

_____
_____
_____

www.iStillLoveMe.com

Focusing on Your Feelings

Since the death, I haven't been able to

_____
_____
_____
_____
_____
_____
_____
_____

Now, I'm having a hard time with

_____
_____
_____
_____
_____
_____
_____
_____

Feelings Journal

Date

And we know that in all things God works for the good of those who love him, who have been called according to his purpose. Romans 8:28 NKJV

I feel sad because

_____
_____
_____
_____
_____
_____

Today I remembered

_____
_____
_____
_____
_____
_____

The things I miss most

_____
_____
_____

www.iStillLoveMe.com

Feelings Journal

Date

Blessed are those who mourn, for they will be comforted. Matthew 5:4 NKJV

I feel sad because

_____
_____
_____
_____
_____

Today I remembered

_____
_____
_____
_____
_____

The things I miss most

_____
_____
_____

Feelings Journal

Date

But Jesus said, "Let the little children come to me and do not hinder them, for to such belongs the kingdom of heaven." Matthew 19:14 NKJV

I feel sad because

_____
_____
_____
_____
_____
_____

Today I remembered

_____
_____
_____
_____
_____
_____

The things I miss most

_____
_____
_____

www.iStillLoveMe.com

My Grief Experience

What does grief feel like for you? In what ways is your grief different than you expected or from others' grief you have observed?

_____
_____
_____
_____
_____
_____
_____
_____
_____
_____
_____
_____
_____
_____
_____
_____
_____
_____
_____
_____
_____
_____
_____
_____

Feelings Journal

Date

Peace I leave with you; my peace I give to you. Not as the world gives do I give to you. Let not your hearts be troubled, neither let them be afraid. John 14:27 NKJV

I feel sad because

_____
_____
_____
_____
_____
_____

Today I remembered

_____
_____
_____
_____
_____
_____

The things I miss most

_____
_____
_____

www.iStillLoveMe.com

Feelings Journal

Date

I have no one else like him, who will show genuine concern for your welfare. Philippians 2:20 NKJV

I feel sad because

_____
_____
_____
_____
_____
_____

Today I remembered

_____
_____
_____
_____
_____
_____

The things I miss most

_____
_____
_____

Feelings Journal

Date

For this God is our God for ever and ever; he will be our guide even to the end. Psalms 48:14 NKJV

I feel sad because

_____
_____
_____
_____
_____
_____

Today I remembered

_____
_____
_____
_____
_____
_____

The things I miss most

_____
_____
_____

www.iStillLoveMe.com

Feelings Journal

Date

Fear not, for I am with you; be not dismayed, for I am your God; I will strengthen you, I will help you, I will uphold you with my righteous right hand.
Isaiah 41:10 NKJV

I feel sad because

_____
_____
_____
_____
_____
_____

Today I remembered

_____
_____
_____
_____
_____
_____

The things I miss most

_____
_____
_____

www.iStillLoveMe.com

Feelings Journal

Date

Who comforts us in all our affliction so that we will be able to comfort those who are in any affliction with the comfort with which we ourselves are comforted by God.
2 Corinthians 1:3-4 NKJV

I feel sad because

_____
_____
_____
_____
_____
_____

Today I remembered

_____
_____
_____
_____
_____
_____

The things I miss most

_____
_____
_____

www.iStillLoveMe.com

Memories

Place pictures below.

www.iStillLoveMe.com

Feelings Journal

Date

For the Lord will not reject forever, For if He causes grief, Then He will have compassion According to His abundant loving kindness. Lamentations 3:31-32 NKJV

I feel sad because

_____
_____
_____
_____
_____
_____

Today I remembered

_____
_____
_____
_____
_____
_____

The things I miss most

_____
_____
_____

Feelings Journal

Date

Therefore you too have grief now; but I will see you again, and your heart will rejoice, and no one will take your joy away from you. John 16:22 NKJV

I feel sad because

_____
_____
_____
_____
_____
_____

Today I remembered

_____
_____
_____
_____
_____
_____

The things I miss most

_____
_____
_____

www.iStillLoveMe.com

Feelings Journal

Date

The LORD also will be a stronghold for the oppressed, A stronghold in times of trouble. Psalms 9:9 NKJV

I feel sad because

___

Today I remembered

___

The things I miss most

___

www.iStillLoveMe.com

Feelings Journal

Date

God is our refuge and strength, A very present help in trouble. Psalms 46:1 NKJV

I feel sad because

_____
_____
_____
_____
_____
_____

Today I remembered

_____
_____
_____
_____
_____
_____

The things I miss most

_____
_____
_____

www.iStillLoveMe.com

Feelings Journal

Date

"O death, where is your victory? O death, where is your sting?" 1 Corinthians 15:55 NKJV

I feel sad because

_____
_____
_____
_____
_____
_____

Today I remembered

_____
_____
_____
_____
_____
_____

The things I miss most

_____
_____
_____

Saying Goodbye

Take time to remember moments of being in the presence of your loved one, and hold in your mind what it felt like to be with them in person.

What do you cherish most about your time together? What do you miss most about being with them, in their presence?

_____
_____
_____
_____
_____
_____
_____
_____
_____
_____
_____
_____
_____
_____
_____
_____
_____
_____
_____
_____

www.iStillLoveMe.com

Feelings Journal

Date

Then I heard a voice from heaven say, "Write this: Blessed are the dead who die in the Lord from now on." "Yes," says the Spirit, "they will rest from their labor, for their deeds will follow them." Revelation 14:13 NKJV

I feel sad because

_____
_____
_____
_____
_____
_____

Today I remembered

_____
_____
_____
_____
_____
_____

The things I miss most

_____
_____
_____

www.iStillLoveMe.com

My Grief Experience

How are you taking care of yourself?

Feelings Journal

Date

Dear friends, now we are children of God, and what we will be has not yet been made known. But we know that when Christ appears, we shall be like him, for we shall see him as he is. 1 John 3:2 NKJV

I feel sad because

_____
_____
_____
_____
_____
_____

Today I remembered

_____
_____
_____
_____
_____
_____

The things I miss most

_____
_____
_____

www.iStillLoveMe.com

Feelings Journal

Date

For I consider that the sufferings of this present time are not worth comparing with the glory that is to be revealed to us. Romans 8:18 NKJV

I feel sad because

_____
_____
_____
_____
_____
_____

Today I remembered

_____
_____
_____
_____
_____
_____

The things I miss most

_____
_____
_____

www.iStillLoveMe.com

Feelings Journal

Date

For they cannot die anymore, because they are equal to angels and are sons of God, being sons of the resurrection. Luke 20:36 NKJV

I feel sad because

_____
_____
_____
_____
_____
_____

Today I remembered

_____
_____
_____
_____
_____
_____

The things I miss most

_____
_____
_____

www.iStillLoveMe.com

Feelings Journal

Date

I shall not die, but live, And declare the works of the Lord. Psalms 118:17 NKJV

I feel sad because

_____
_____
_____
_____
_____
_____

Today I remembered

_____
_____
_____
_____
_____
_____

The things I miss most

_____
_____
_____

www.iStillLoveMe.com

Feelings Journal

Date

"Grief is a curious thing, when it happens unexpectedly. It is a band-aid being ripped away, taking the top layer off a family. And the underbelly of a household is never pretty, ours no exception." - Jodi Picoult

I feel sad because

_____
_____
_____
_____
_____
_____

Today I remembered

_____
_____
_____
_____
_____
_____

The things I miss most

_____
_____
_____

www.iStillLoveMe.com

Feelings Journal

Date

"How lucky I am to have something that makes saying goodbye so hard." - Winnie the Pooh

I feel sad because

_____
_____
_____
_____
_____
_____

Today I remembered

_____
_____
_____
_____
_____
_____

The things I miss most

_____
_____
_____

Feelings Journal

Date

Rejoice in the Lord always. Again I will say, rejoice!
Philippians 4:4 NKJV

I feel sad because

_____
_____
_____
_____
_____
_____

Today I remembered

_____
_____
_____
_____
_____
_____

The things I miss most

_____
_____
_____

www.iStillLoveMe.com

Feelings Journal

Date

"Grieving doesn't make you imperfect. It makes you human." - Sarah Dessen

I feel sad because

_____
_____
_____
_____
_____
_____

Today I remembered

_____
_____
_____
_____
_____
_____

The things I miss most

_____
_____
_____

www.iStillLoveMe.com

Feelings Journal

Date

Now may the God of hope fill you with all joy and peace in believing, that you may abound in hope by the power of the Holy Spirit. Romans 15:13 NKJV

I feel sad because

_____
_____
_____
_____
_____
_____

Today I remembered

_____
_____
_____
_____
_____
_____

The things I miss most

_____
_____
_____

www.iStillLoveMe.com

Memories

Place pictures below.

www.iStillLoveMe.com

I wish I could tell you...

Write a letter to your loved one about all that's happened in your life after they left...

Feelings Journal

Date

"Never. We never lose our loved ones. They accompany us; they don't disappear from our lives. We are merely in different rooms." - Paulo Coelho

I feel sad because

_____
_____
_____
_____
_____
_____

Today I remembered

_____
_____
_____
_____
_____
_____

The things I miss most

_____
_____
_____

Releasing The Guilt

What did you expect of yourself that you were not able to do?

_____
_____
_____

Were those expectations realistic?

_____
_____
_____

Would your loved one forgive you now? What do you suppose your deceased loved one would say to you in this situation?

_____
_____
_____

What have you learned from this mistake that you can apply to your current life?

_____
_____
_____

www.iStillLoveMe.com

Feelings Journal

Date

But the fruit of the Spirit is love, joy, peace, longsuffering, kindness, goodness, faithfulness, gentleness, self-control. Against such there is no law. Galatians 5:22-23 NKJV

I feel sad because

_____
_____
_____
_____
_____
_____

Today I remembered

_____
_____
_____
_____
_____
_____

The things I miss most

_____
_____
_____

www.iStillLoveMe.com

Feelings Journal

Date

Until now you have asked nothing in My name. Ask, and you will receive, that your joy may be full.
John 16:24 NKJV

I feel sad because

_____
_____
_____
_____
_____
_____

Today I remembered

_____
_____
_____
_____
_____
_____

The things I miss most

_____
_____
_____

www.iStillLoveMe.com

Feelings Journal

Date

You will show me the path of life; In Your presence is fullness of joy; At Your right hand are pleasures forevermore. Psalms 16:11 NKJV

I feel sad because

_____
_____
_____
_____
_____
_____

Today I remembered

_____
_____
_____
_____
_____
_____

The things I miss most

_____
_____
_____

www.iStillLoveMe.com

Feelings Journal

Date

For the kingdom of God is not eating and drinking, but righteousness and peace and joy in the Holy Spirit.
Romans 14:17 NKJV

I feel sad because

_____
_____
_____
_____
_____
_____

Today I remembered

_____
_____
_____
_____
_____
_____

The things I miss most

_____
_____
_____

Memories

Place pictures below.

www.iStillLoveMe.com

Releasing The Hurt

What are you holding on to?

_____
_____
_____

In what way does your past prevent you from moving forward?

_____
_____
_____

How will you move forward?

_____
_____
_____

What are you willing to release?

_____
_____
_____

Feelings Journal

Date

Whom having not seen you love. Though now you do not see Him, yet believing, you rejoice with joy inexpressible and full of glory. 1 Peter 1:8 NKJV

I feel sad because

_____
_____
_____
_____
_____
_____

Today I remembered

_____
_____
_____
_____
_____
_____

The things I miss most

_____
_____
_____

www.iStillLoveMe.com

Feelings Journal

Date

In the multitude of my anxieties within me, Your comforts delight my soul. Psalms 94:19 NKJV

I feel sad because

_____
_____
_____
_____
_____
_____

Today I remembered

_____
_____
_____
_____
_____
_____

The things I miss most

_____
_____
_____

www.iStillLoveMe.com

Feelings Journal

Date

You have turned for me my mourning into dancing; You have put off my sackcloth and clothed me with gladness. Psalms 30:11 NKJV

I feel sad because

_____
_____
_____
_____
_____
_____

Today I remembered

_____
_____
_____
_____
_____
_____

The things I miss most

_____
_____
_____

Feelings Journal

Date

For our heart shall rejoice in Him, Because we have trusted in His holy name. Psalms 33:21 NKJV

I feel sad because

_____
_____
_____
_____
_____
_____

Today I remembered

_____
_____
_____
_____
_____
_____

The things I miss most

_____
_____
_____

www.iStillLoveMe.com

My Grief Experience

Do you find that some words trigger an emotional response?

_____
_____
_____
_____
_____
_____
_____
_____
_____
_____
_____
_____
_____
_____
_____
_____
_____
_____
_____
_____
_____
_____

Feelings Journal

Date

"Without you in my arms, I feel an emptiness in my soul. I find myself searching the crowds for your face - I know it's an impossibility, but I cannot help myself." - Nicholas Sparks

I feel sad because

_____
_____
_____
_____
_____
_____

Today I remembered

_____
_____
_____
_____
_____
_____

The things I miss most

_____
_____
_____

www.iStillLoveMe.com

Feelings Journal

Date

For our light and momentary troubles are achieving for us an eternal glory that far outweighs them all. So we fix our eyes not on what is seen, but on what is unseen, since what is seen is temporary, but what is unseen is eternal.
2 Corinthians 4:17-18 NKJV

I feel sad because

_____
_____
_____
_____
_____
_____

Today I remembered

_____
_____
_____
_____
_____

The things I miss most

_____
_____
_____

www.iStillLoveMe.com

Feelings Journal

Date

Have I not commanded you? Be strong and courageous. Do not be afraid; do not be discouraged, for the LORD your God will be with you wherever you go.
Joshua 1:9 NKJV

I feel sad because

_____
_____
_____
_____
_____

Today I remembered

_____
_____
_____
_____
_____

The things I miss most

_____
_____
_____

www.iStillLoveMe.com

Feelings Journal

Date

After that, we who are still alive and are left will be caught up together with them in the clouds to meet the Lord in the air. And so we will be with the Lord forever. Therefore encourage one another with these words.
1 Thessalonians 4:17-18 NKJV

I feel sad because

_____
_____
_____
_____
_____
_____

Today I remembered

_____
_____
_____
_____
_____
_____

The things I miss most

_____
_____
_____

www.iStillLoveMe.com

Feelings Journal

Date

The righteous perish, and no one takes it to heart; the devout are taken away, and no one understands that the righteous are taken away to be spared from evil. Those who walk uprightly enter into peace; they find rest as they lie in death.
Isaiah 57:1-2 NKJV

I feel sad because

_____
_____
_____
_____
_____
_____

Today I remembered

_____
_____
_____
_____
_____
_____

The things I miss most

_____
_____
_____

www.iStillLoveMe.com

My Grief Experience

Do you feel you've had to hide some of your grief?

_____
_____
_____
_____
_____
_____
_____
_____
_____
_____
_____
_____
_____
_____
_____
_____
_____
_____
_____
_____
_____
_____
_____
_____

Feelings Journal

Date

Then he said to them, "Go your way. Eat the fat and drink sweet wine and send portions to anyone who has nothing ready, for this day is holy to our Lord. And do not be grieved, for the joy of the Lord is your strength." Nehemiah 8:10 NKJV

I feel sad because

_____
_____
_____
_____
_____
_____

Today I remembered

_____
_____
_____
_____
_____
_____

The things I miss most

_____
_____
_____

www.iStillLoveMe.com

Feelings Journal

Date

I have set the Lord always before me; Because He is at my right hand I shall not be moved. Therefore my heart is glad, and my glory rejoices; My flesh also will rest in hope.
Psalms 16:8-9 NKJV

I feel sad because

_____
_____
_____
_____
_____
_____

Today I remembered

_____
_____
_____
_____
_____
_____

The things I miss most

_____
_____
_____

www.iStillLoveMe.com

Feelings Journal

Date

The reality is that you will grieve forever. You will not 'get over' the loss of a loved one; you'll learn to live with it. You will heal and you will rebuild yourself around the loss you have suffered. You will be whole again but you will never be the same. Nor should you be the same nor would you want to." - Elizabeth Kubler-Ross + David Kessler

I feel sad because

_____
_____
_____
_____
_____
_____

Today I remembered

_____
_____
_____
_____
_____
_____

The things I miss most

_____
_____
_____

www.iStillLoveMe.com

Feelings Journal

Date

You Shall Live!

I feel sad because

___

Today I remembered

___

The things I miss most

___

www.iStillLoveMe.com

Effects of Grief

How has your loss affected you?

COGNITIVE ABILITIES	EMOTIONS

BODY	SPIRITUAL BELIEFS

www.iStillLoveMe.com

Feelings Journal

Date

It's okay to not be okay!

I feel sad because

_____
_____
_____
_____
_____
_____

Today I remembered

_____
_____
_____
_____
_____
_____

The things I miss most

_____
_____
_____

www.iStillLoveMe.com

Working towards Acceptance

What does acceptance mean to you?

_____
_____
_____
_____
_____
_____
_____
_____

Where are you in your acceptance? Draw a line or X below.

Self-talk: write down some things you could say to yourself to practice acceptance.

_____
_____
_____
_____
_____
_____
_____
_____
_____

Don't leave it unsaid...

Write a letter to your loved one about all the ways they made you feel loved and supported during their life.

Grief Affirmations

Use the templates below and create your affirmations that will help you to cope with grief and loss.

I am _____

I allow myself to _____

I let go of _____

I'm surrounded by _____

I accept _____

I can _____

I am thankful for _____

I have _____

It's okay for me to _____

I focus on _____

I take comfort in _____

I will be _____

www.iStillLoveMe.com

Express Yourself

Date

Express Yourself

Date

Express Yourself

Date

Express Yourself

Date

www.iStillLoveMe.com

Express Yourself

Date

Express Yourself

Date

www.iStillLoveMe.com

Express Yourself

Date

Express Yourself

Date

Express Yourself

Date

Express Yourself

Date

Express Yourself

Date

Express Yourself

Date

Express Yourself

Date

Express Yourself

Date

Express Yourself

Date

Express Yourself

Date

Express Yourself

Date

Express Yourself

Date

www.iStillLoveMe.com

Express Yourself

Date

Express Yourself

Date

Express Yourself

Date

Express Yourself

Date

Express Yourself

Date

Express Yourself

Date

Express Yourself

Date

Express Yourself

Date

Express Yourself

Date

www.iStillLoveMe.com

Express Yourself

Date

Express Yourself

Date

Express Yourself

Date

Express Yourself

Date

Express Yourself

Date

Express Yourself

Date

Express Yourself

Date

Express Yourself

Date

Express Yourself

Date

Express Yourself

Date

www.iStillLoveMe.com

Express Yourself

Date

Express Yourself

Date

Express Yourself

Date

Express Yourself

Date

Express Yourself

Date

Express Yourself

Date

Express Yourself

Date

Express Yourself

Date

Express Yourself

Date

Express Yourself

Date

Express Yourself

Date

Express Yourself

Date

Express Yourself

Date

Express Yourself

Date

The Grief Coach

Arletha Orr is a profound speaker with a purpose to inspire and impact her audience. She is dedicated to consciously shifting the way we live. It was only when her world collapsed around her, after a fatal evening that Arletha discovered her true calling in life.

She knew that God had a greater purpose for her and with Him by her side, Orr began her journey to shine a light for the people whose lives had been consumed by the darkness around them.

With her passion and vigor, she hopes to selflessly serve others and save souls for God's Kingdom. Orr is an Author and Publisher. She's also a Certified Grief Coach who has answered the call of God on her life to inspire and encourage those around her.

Thank You!

We would love to hear from you! Send comments and suggestions to hello@arlethaorr.com.

Stay Connected!

- **f** Arletha Orr
- **◉** thegriefcoachms
- **◉** thegriefcoachms

www.iShallLive.com
www.iStillLoveMe.com

Grieving in the Holy Ghost is a guided grief journal that lets you process your grief while memory keeping. Each part was designed to help you walk through your journey while also allowing you to commemorate and honor your loved one.

The guided scriptures and tools will help you gain strength and courage to live a life of freedom!

Arletha is an American Author from Mississippi who loves serving others. Better known as "The Grief Coach," she has answered the call of God on her life to inspire and encourage those around her.

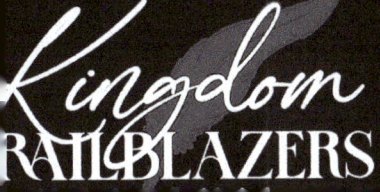

www.ingramcontent.com/pod-product-compliance
Lightning Source LLC
Chambersburg PA
CBHW060654060526
44119CB00076B/249